The Great Piano ~~Works Of~~
SERGEI RACHMANINOFF

WARNER BROS. PUBLICATIONS - THE GLOBAL LEADER IN PRINT
USA: 15800 NW 48th Avenue, Miami, FL 33014

WARNER/CHAPPELL MUSIC

CANADA: 40 SHEPPARD AVE. WEST, SUITE 800
TORONTO, ONTARIO, M2N 6K9
SCANDINAVIA: P.O. BOX 533, VENDEVAGEN 85 B
S-182 15, DANDERYD, SWEDEN
AUSTRALIA: P.O. BOX 353
3 TALAVERA ROAD, NORTH RYDE N.S.W. 2113

NUOVA CARISCH

ITALY: VIA CAMPANIA, 12
20098 S. GIULIANO MILANESE (MI)
ZONA INDUSTRIALE SESTO ULTERIANO
SPAIN: MAGALLANES, 25
28015 MADRID
FRANCE: 20, RUE DE LA VILLE-L'EVEQUE, 75008 PARIS

IMP
INTERNATIONAL MUSIC PUBLICATIONS LIMITED

ENGLAND: GRIFFIN HOUSE,
161 HAMMERSMITH ROAD, LONDON W6 8BS
GERMANY: MARSTALLSTR. 8, D-80539 MUNCHEN
DENMARK: DANMUSIK, VOGNMAGERGADE 7
DK 1120 KOBENHAVNK

Project Manager: Dale Tucker
Design: Michael Ramsay

699

SERGEI RACHMANINOFF
Born: April 1, 1873, Oneg, Russia
Died: March 28, 1943, Beverly Hills, California

Sergei Rachmaninoff was born into a wealthy, influential family on an estate in Russia. His father was captain of the Russian Imperial Guard, and his mother a talented musician. She began teaching music to Rachmaninoff when he was only a few years old, and he showed great talent quickly.

When Rachmaninoff was ten, the family had a severe financial setback and moved to St. Petersburg. There, he entered the St. Petersburg Conservatory, studied under Demiansky, and quickly surpassed his classmates. However, he did not enjoy practicing or studying, and often missed classes. He was sent to the Moscow Conservatory where he lived with his teacher, Nicolai Zverev. Zverev was a strict teacher and enforcer of practice habits, and thus Rachmaninoff progressed rapidly. He won honors as a pianist, but also achieved a growing respect as a composer during this period. The Prelude in C sharp Minor was composed when Rachmaninoff was only nineteen, and this piece brought him world-wide fame.

1897 saw the premiere of Rachmaninoff's first Symphony; however, a bad performance left him embarassed. It is said he fled the concert hall and destroyed the score. The torment of this eventually led to a nervous breakdown. After counselling, Rachmaninoff recovered, went back to composing, and was reestablished with the premiere of his second Piano Concerto, one of the most often performed concertos even today.

He was later appointed the conductor of the Moscow Grand Theatre Orchestra, and continued to gain fame as a virtuoso pianist. He married his cousin in 1902, had a daughter, and shortly thereafter moved his family to Dresden to attain a more peaceful environment in which to compose.

In 1909 Rachmaninoff made his first concert tour to the United States where he premiered his third Piano Concerto. This tour was a tremendous success, and laid the groundwork for future tours. When the Bolshevik Revolution began in 1917, Rachmaninoff left Russia, moving to Switzerland, and then to New York in 1935. He later moved to Los Angeles, but never returned to Russia again. His music, however, contained his love of the Russian heritage, as did his American home.

Rachmaninoff's later years were filled with concert tours, where he was always greeted positively, and he continued composing. On the thirtieth anniversary of his first trip to America, major music festivals were held in New York and Philadelphia at which he conducted and played the piano in concerts of his own music. His final tour was in early 1943, but failing health forced him to return to California before completing the concerts. He became an American citizen in March of that year and died only a few weeks later, leaving behind a wealth of beautiful music reminiscent of his native Russia.

CONTENTS

EIGHTEENTH VARIATION
from "Rhapsodie on a Theme of Paganini"

SERGEI RACHMANINOFF
Adapted for Piano Solo by
Hermene W. Eichorn

to Monsieur A. Arensky

PRELUDE IN C SHARP MINOR
Opus 3, No. 2

PRELUDE
Opus 23, No. 4

PRELUDE
Opus 23, No. 5

Alla marcia

18

Un poco meno mosso.

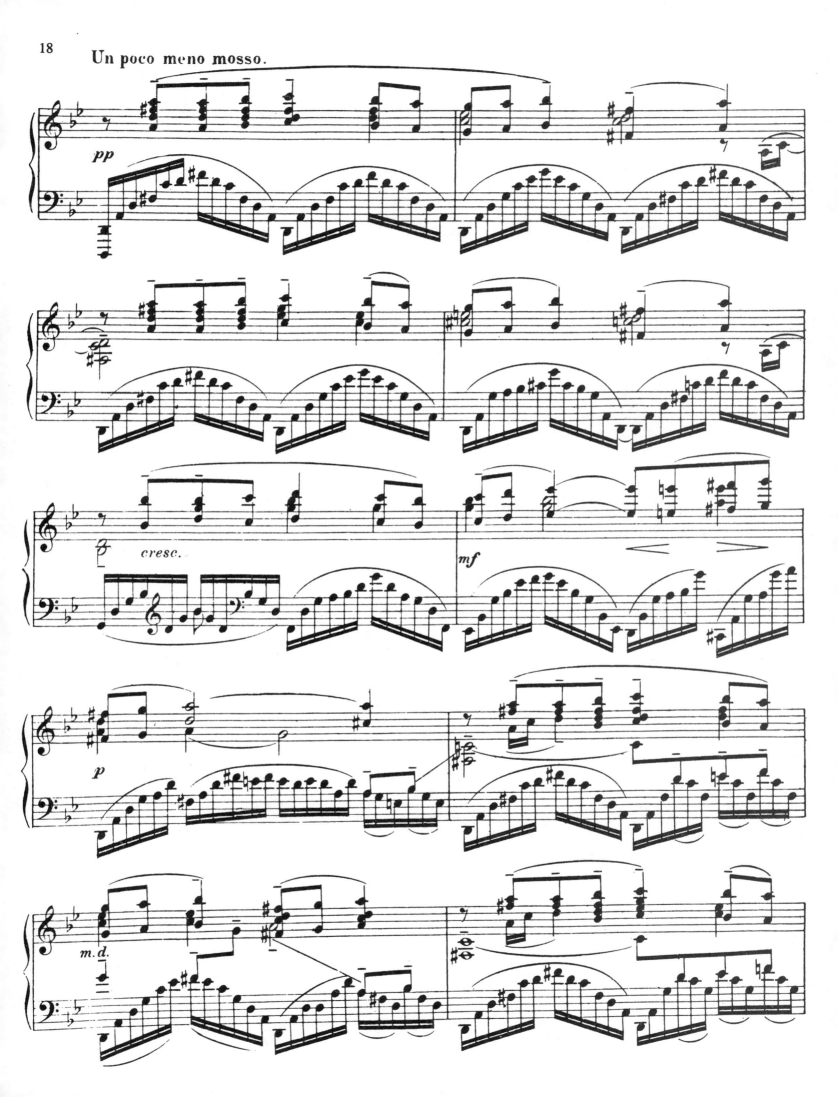

poco a poco accelerando e cresc. al Tempo I

PRELUDE
Opus 23, No. 10

PRELUDE
Opus 32, No. 4

PRELUDE
Opus 32, No. 11

THE BUMBLE-BEE

NICOLAI RIMSKY-KORSAKOV
Transcribed by Sergei Rachmaninoff

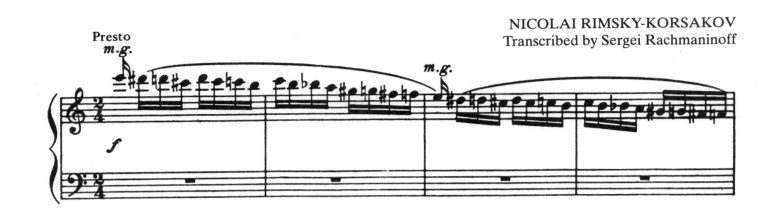

MINUET
from "L' Arlésienne Suite"

GEORGES BIZET
Transcribed by Sergei Rachmaninoff

Tempo di Minuetto

Con pedale

45

LIEBESLIED
Love's Sorrow

FRITZ KREISLER
Transcribed by Sergei Rachmaninoff

53

p grazioso e dolce

57

LIEBESFREUD
Love's Joy

FRITZ KREISLER
Transcribed by Sergei Rachmaninoff

e grazioso

68

Presto

PIECE IN D MINOR

to Monsieur A. Arensky

ELÉGIE
Opus 3, No. 1

MÉLODIE
Opus 3, No. 3

*As revised by
the composer*

87

LILACS
Opus 21, No. 5

Revised and as played
by the composer

to Monsieur A. Arensky

SÉRÉNADE
Opus 3, No. 5

94

MELODIE
Opus 10, No. 4

VALSE
Opus 10, No. 2

104

BARCAROLLE
Opus 10, No. 3

Con moto

ROMANCE
Opus 10, No. 6

MOMENT MUSICAL
Opus 16, No. 3

Andante cantabile

MOMENT MUSICAL
Opus 16, No. 5

NOCTURNE
Opus 10, No. 1

Andante espressivo

132

ETUDE-TABLEAU
Opus 33, No. 1

ETUDE-TABLEAU
Opus 33, No. 7

Allegro con fuoco
molto marcato

ETUDE-TABLEAU
Opus 33, No. 8

ETUDE-TABLEAU
Opus 39, No. 2

ETUDE-TABLEAU
Opus 39, No. 8

to Monsieur Th. Leschetizky

VARIATIONS
on a Theme of Chopin
Opus 22

THEME
F. Chopin
Op. 28, No. 20
Largo

160

Var. V
Meno mosso (♩ = 92)

Var. XI
Lento (♩.= 44)

Var. XII
Moderato (♩ = 60)

Var. XV
Allegro scherzando (♩.= 132)

Var. XVI
Lento (♩=54)

Var. XVII
Grave (♩ = 46)

Var. XVIII
Più mosso

Var. XIX
Allegro vivace

Var. XX
Presto (♩.= 92)

Var. XXII

Maestoso (♩= 100)

Presto